POWER IN
Knowledge

JERRI WOOD

Power in Knowledge
Copyright © 2023 by Jerri Wood

ISBN: 979-8988147176 (sc)
ISBN: 979-8988147183 (e)

Riverview Press

info@riverview-press.com
www.riverview-press.com

2 Peter 1:3

His divine power has given us everything we need for a godly life through our knowledge of him who called us by his own glory and goodness.

This book is written to show that the more knowledge we have the closer we can live to our Savior. The above verse says His divine power has given us everything we need. Our knowledge of Him will help us live a godly life. He has called us. Are we listening?

SUMMARY

Throughout this book I have attempted to help you understand that having knowledge of God's Word is necessary to living our Christian lives. The more knowledge we have the better able to serve Jesus we will be.

There is power in knowing Him and what His Word says to us. This book would be good for a group Bible study because the chapters are topical in nature. It could also be used as a devotional for individuals. The truths are the same for both groups. When we encounter storms in life, or need to know about God's unfailing love, or that we are fragile jars of clay just trying to do what Jesus wants us to do, we will find help in His Word.

Scripture references are NIV unless otherwise stated in the reading.

My prayer for you is that in the reading of this book you will grow to trust His heart and lean on Him for everything. He is in control, don't you forget that!

DEDICATION

This book is dedicated to God. Without Him there would be no book. He is All in All to me.

ACKNOWLEDGEMENT

I have to give credit to all the good people who have helped me out during the writing of this book as well as the publishing.

To my publisher Rosemary who continues to always encourage me and give me pointers, while helping me edit.

To Pat Ravenscraft, my friend, who helps me edit and keeps me on track.

To my lovely sister Judy Woltz who reads for me and gives me ideas of items to include in my lessons. To all the wonderful people who sent me their stories for me to include in my Glimpses of God chapter.

To my daughter Stephanie Remington for letting me give her my ideas for cover design and then taking it and making it something beautiful!

To my husband for the support he gives me when I go out on a limb for God! Most of all to God for his unfailing love and mercy to me!

Thank you isn't enough, but thank you!

TABLE OF CONTENTS

CHAPTER 1

Our Story-God's Miracle

It seems that both times I started writing a book which I feel God has called me to write, things start happening! If you read my book, "Power in Stillness," you will recall we had a huge plumbing issue. This book seems to be starting out the same way!

Here is what happened. We got scammed on our computer, and I mean scammed big time! I won't go into all the details except to tell you it was a substantial amount of money! Talk about a shock! I immediately started praying and asking God to help us figure this out. I also asked others to pray as well. Our Pastor called and prayed with my husband. We called out the prayer warriors! That was the first and best thing we could have done. You will see why as I work through this chapter.

This thing came to a head on Thursday evening. You can probably imagine the prayers going up and the feeling of powerlessness we had. I will say that I slept relatively well, which was my first clue that God was working! When I got up on Friday morning, I just knew that God had something for me. What I want to talk the most about in this chapter is how He dealt with me through all of this. I want you to see the promises He gave me on Friday morning. I wrote them in my journal because I knew that God knew I was going to need some things to give me comfort to get me through this. God did not disappoint!

The following are some of my journal entries from Thursday evening to the resolution of this crazy thing on Friday! God is just amazing!

> Thursday evening: "And so it begins; we got scammed! Every time I say I'm going to write, something happens! God, I'm trusting You to fix this!"

> Friday morning: "I can't wait to see what God has for me this morning!"

I really felt like this on Friday morning. I just had a feeling that He had something He was going to tell me that was wonderful. I was right! During my quiet time here is what God gave me, Isaiah 49:13-16 TNIV:

> "Shout for joy, you heavens: rejoice you earth; burst into song, you mountains! For the LORD comforts his people and will have compassion on his afflicted ones. But Zion said, 'The LORD has forgotten me, the LORD has forgotten me.

> Can a mother forget the baby at her breast and have no compassion on the child she has borne? Though she may forget, I will not forget you!' See, I have engraved you on the palm of my hands; your walls are ever before me."

That was very special and timely, and God knew exactly what I needed. I needed to know that He hadn't forgotten me. He knew that I was feeling afflicted, and He was bringing comfort! But that wasn't all. The next thing I wrote in my journal was something I had thought the night before.

> I had spoken in two different places recently and the gist of the message was this: STOP, S-Seek Him, T-Trust His Heart, O-Obey His Word P-Persevere. Okay, I'm thinking, practice what you preach, Jerri!

When I got up on Friday morning, one of the ladies who had heard me speak, reminded me of S.T.O.P! I got the message, so I continued to seek God and see what else He had for me. A devotional book I'm using right now quoted 1 Chronicles 16:11:

> "Look to the LORD and His strength; seek His face always."

Another passage I read was Psalm 121 TNIV:

> "I lift up my eyes to the mountains, where does my help come from? My help comes from the LORD, the maker of heaven and earth. He <u>will not</u> let your foot slip-he who watches over you will not slumber, indeed, he who watches over Israel will neither slumber nor sleep.

> The LORD watches over you-the LORD is your shade at your right hand; the sun will not harm you by day, nor the moon by night.

> The LORD will keep you from <u>all</u> harm He will watch over your life; the LORD will watch over your coming and going both <u>now</u> and forevermore."

Wow! God kept telling me over and over in His Word that He was taking care of us. I'm so thankful for His Word. It's where I run to when I need help!

There are still more verses to come:

> Joshua 1:9 (TNIV): "Have I not commanded you? Be strong and courageous. Do not be afraid; do not be discouraged, for the LORD your God will be with you wherever you go."

You may think I specifically looked these up, but that is not the case. Some of these I had underlined in my Bible, but others of these passages were in my devotional reading for this day! God knows ahead of time what we need and brings it to us for His purposes and when He knows we will need the help.

Another verse is in Psalm 119:76:

> "May your unfailing love be my comfort according to your promise to your servant."

All along this morning's journey, God kept assuring me of His love and goodness. Then He brought me to a really cool verse Zechariah 9:12:

> "Return to your fortress, you prisoner of hope; even now I announce that I will restore twice as much to you."

My prayer to that was:

> "I don't know how, Lord, but I'm choosing to believe You and trust You!"

When I looked up the part about twice as much, I found that it means He will fully restore! I didn't even want twice as much, I just wanted what was stolen from us to be given back! How amazing!

The next verse God gave me came from Zechariah 2: 8-9

> For this is what the LORD Almighty says: "After the Glorious One has sent me against the nations that have plundered you-for whoever touches you touches the apple of his eye- I will surely raise my hand against them so that their slaves will plunder them. Then you will know that the LORD Almighty has sent me."

I surely felt plundered, but God was in control!

Isn't it amazing how God had all these scriptures lined out for me? I have one more scripture, but first I want to fill in some of the day's events on Friday. Since all of this happened, of course, we had to put a stop on our banking. I had stopped at the bank to get cash and was talking to the manager. He was sorry about what had happened and was up front in telling me there was only a slim chance of ever seeing that money again. I told him that a slim chance was better than zero chance and that God was in control. It would be okay. He agreed, but I could tell he wasn't buying it!

In the meantime, my husband had been talking to the fraud department about our situation. The guy he spoke with said he thought there was almost no chance of ever seeing the money. So, at this point things were looking bleak, at least as far as the world was concerned.

But God…

God had other plans. You see, God had given me all these promises. He had helped me and blessed me with just a small amount of faith. Enough for me to tell my daughter I was still holding out hope during the afternoon on Friday!

Not even 15 minutes passed when we got a call from our banker that we were getting our money back! EVERY. SINGLE. PENNY! I went around my house shouting Praise the Lord! Thank You, Jesus! Oh, my goodness! God had prevailed against all odds! What a miracle!

We had to go back to the bank on Friday, right after they called, to sign a paper. I didn't have to go along, but I wanted to, so I could see the bank manager again. The first thing I said when I saw him was, "What did I say to you this morning? God is in control!" He just kind of shook his head. I know he thinks I'm crazy, but I don't care! I know exactly Who got our money back! Woo Hoo!

Here is the last set of verses that God gave me four years ago when we moved into our present house. Haggai 2:8-10: TNIV.

> "The silver is mine and the gold is mine, declares the LORD Almighty. The glory of this present house will be greater than the glory of the former house," says the LORD Almighty. "And in this place, I will grant peace," declares the LORD Almighty.

I believe this verse still holds true today for me and my house!

> On Saturday morning here is what I wrote in my journal first thing. "Praise God from whom all blessings flow. Praise Him all creatures here below. Praise Him above ye heavenly host. Praise Father, Son, and Holy Ghost!

> God has worked out all the mess and gotten all our money back! I just can't praise Him enough! Thank You Jesus, for your promises

to me yesterday. Thank you for the hope you gave me, even though it seemed very small.

Against all odds You took care of us. We had two different people tell us we'd probably never see that money ever again. Hah! They were wrong, God had other plans!"

Through this I got to witness to the people at the bank, to folks on Facebook, to people at church and now to all of you! God is amazing, just amazing!

I had to go back in the bank a few days after all this and again I saw the bank manager. I spoke to him briefly and said, "It truly was a miracle!" and he had to agree! Praise God for miracles! They do happen!

CHAPTER 2

Biblical Flowers - Are You Growing?

I love flowers! Each flower is made in such a unique way that there seems to be no end to all the different types. "The National Science Foundation's current estimates place the number of known plant species at more than 400,000."[1] Not only that, but this number keeps changing because about "2,000 new species are identified every year!"[1]

Some flowers smell wonderful, while some have a bad smell and others have no smell at all. They range in every color of the rainbow and are used for lots of different purposes. In this lesson, I want to talk about a few of the different flowers mentioned in the Bible.

The first flower to be discussed is the lily. "These are the wild field flowers in Palestine and almost certainly the wild anemone that were referred to by Jesus as the lilies of the field in His sermon on the Mount, as they still grow wild near the Lake of Galilee."[2]

Can you picture Jesus walking in the field and stooping to pick this flower? These lilies are not the type of lily we may picture when we think of lilies! It is similar in looks to a poppy and has a wide range of colors, such as red, purple, and white. I'm sure when he picked it up, it caught people's attention.

Let's look at what Jesus has to say in Matthew 6:28, "And why worry about your clothing? Look at the lilies of the field and how they grow. They don't work or make their clothing." He went on to say that even Solomon wasn't dressed as well as that lily! It is a beautiful flower! These lilies bloom in the spring which is about the time of the year when it is believed that Jesus gave His sermon on the Mount. Some writers think the flowers could have included many different types of wildflowers that grew on the hillside. At any rate, Jesus was using an everyday object to make a point - something He was very good at.

Another flower is the daffodil mentioned in Song of Solomon 2:1 and Isaiah 35:1-2. Sometimes these are translated as Rose of Sharon or crocus. It is hard to know the exact kind of flowers in the Bible because the people writing the books were more interested in the gist of the message.

The crocus sativus or saffron crocus is another type of flower mentioned. This flower is really interesting. It takes over 4,000 crocus flowers to produce one ounce of saffron. The powder made from the upper end of the style is used to flavor cakes, stews and curries. It is listed in Song of Solomon 4:14 along with lots of other spices, such as myrrh, cinnamon, nard, calamus, and aloe. Although some of these are not flowers, they are plants and that is what I want to focus on next.

So, what is it that plants and flowers need to grow? There are three things, water, light and soil that are needed if you plan to try your hand at gardening. We are going to look at these aspects first from a physical point of view, then move to the spiritual aspect. So, here goes!

First, we all know that plants need water. Depending on the type of plant, you must give your plant just the right amount. Some plants require a lot of water and others just a small amount. Not enough will kill off a plant for sure, but overwatering will too! Who hasn't killed a cactus by giving it too much water? We must be sure to give each individual plant just the right amount.

So, are you starting to make spiritual connections here? What do we as Christian's need to grow? Let's look at water again from a spiritual perspective. In John 4:14 (TNIV) Jesus said this, "But those who drink the water I give them will never thirst. Indeed, the water I give them will become in them a spring of water welling up to eternal life." In essence, Jesus is telling us we need HIM! He is the Living Water. If we don't have Him, we will die, just like a plant does if it is not watered. So, how do we get this water if we are a Christian? Read the Word, talk to Him, nurture your relationship with Him. If you only watered your plant once a month, would you be able to keep it alive? I don't think so. We must have the right amount of water. Some cacti can store water for up to two years! We cannot! We are not in the cactus family; we MUST have the Living Water every day to remain alive and well.

On to the second thing plants and flowers need, and that is light. If you grow violets, you know they need indirect light. If they were in full sunlight, they would wither. Some plants, however, need lots of sun. Some need shade for most of the day to grow properly. I've recently learned about "hardening off" a plant. This means that baby plants raised in a greenhouse must be acclimated before putting them outside. This toughens them up, so they don't die due to the harshness of the sun and wind. I didn't do this with a package of seeds I had grown in the house. When I took them outside, every one of them died. Lesson learned.

Just as plants need light to flourish, so do we need the Light only God can give. What am I talking about here? John 1:9 says that Jesus is the true light, that He is the One who gives light to everyone. I like the way The Amplified Bible states it. "There it was - the true Light (the genuine, perfect, steadfast Light) which coming into the world, enlightens everyone." Remember those baby plants that needed to be toughened up? We as Christians need to be toughened as well. We need to have Jesus' light to make us strong.

The third thing plants need is soil. Some like sandy soil, others need acidic soil. Some plants even appear to grow in rocks, although I'm sure there must be soil in there somewhere! Some are planted deep while others are not.

If a plant is not planted deep enough it will not grow well. I have the perfect example of this in my flower bed. For some reason when I planted my bedding plants this spring there were a couple that I didn't get deep enough. You know how I can tell? Because they are dying! They didn't grow beautiful flowers on them, they are just not healthy enough. You know what happened as a result of me writing this? I went out to the flower bed and bunched up some soil around those plants and the next time I went out to check on them, one of them had grown a flower! Isn't that the most amazing thing? You know, God will do that for us as well if we will just let Him! Just like plants, if we don't get grounded (planted deep enough in Jesus) we will wither as well!

In Matthew 14:5-8 it talks about the seeds that fell on rocky places. If there is not enough soil the plant may start growing well, but when the environment becomes too harsh, the plant will die. Sometimes, the plant doesn't get a good enough root to help it be successful. Sometimes that happens to people too! If we are living for Jesus, we need to be aware of our environment. If we don't take time to learn His Word and hear from Him, we will suffer from the harshness of this world. This is why we need to be toughened up with God's Word, which goes back to the amount of light we need! You see, all three of these things work together. Without any one of them our plants will not be successful, and neither will we be in our Christian walk if we neglect any of these things! We must have the Word and get planted deep to survive!

I hope you are receiving Jesus' Light, Water and Soil, but what if you aren't? Are there some things you can do to change that? I'm glad you asked! Because there are some steps you can take to make a difference in your life. Maybe you are just doing okay, but not great, and you'd like things to be better between you and God. Maybe you don't know God. Maybe you need that relationship to deepen. I hope the following suggestions will help you grow deeper in your walk with Jesus.

The first thing to do is remove yourself. Get away from everything. Find a time in your day when you can be alone. Just you and God. I know this can be hard, especially when you have little ones, or a job, or both! I've been there! I was a teacher for many years. When my girls were little, I had to use their nap time as my quiet time. As they got older, and I started working, my time was earlier in the morning.

I've heard some women say they got up at 4:00 a.m. That's a little much for me! I need to be able to be awake when I seek God. I don't want to miss anything pertinent, you know! Anyway, what I'm saying is, carve out some time in your day to receive light, instruction, help, hope, peace and joy. Your life will change because of it!

Even Jesus, who was perfect, had to find time alone with His Father. Let's look at Luke 5:16 (TNIV), "But Jesus <u>often</u>

withdrew to lonely places and prayed." Now, I don't know about you, but if Jesus thought this was an important thing to do, maybe we should think about it too!

Not only should we try to make this time alone with God a priority and a time to bring our requests to Him, but we also need to be listening. If you are reading your Bible and praying and really thinking about what you are doing, the Holy Spirit will speak to you. He will guide you, give you advice, give you comfort, give you peace. That's what this relationship is all about. God wants to hear from you, but He also has things He wants to tell you. He has trouble doing that if you are never listening!

So, besides light, soil and water, what are some other things that keep plants from growing? Well, we've already said, location, location, location. If you put a plant in the wrong environment, it will not be successful. Think about a cactus outside in Missouri in the wintertime. It would do okay for a time in the summer, but winter weather would kill it off. Think about your environment. Where are you spending your time? What are you doing while you are there? Are you allowing sinful things to enter your realm? Or are you filling your area with praise and worship? Just something to think about!

Another thing that will keep a plant from growing is being a knothead! A knothead is a rosebud that won't open and become beautiful. Don't be like a knothead. God wants to make you beautiful inside and out! If you will let Him, He will transform you into the most beautiful of flowers!

The last thing that will keep you from growing is watching what you sow. What am I referring to here? If you plant roses, you get roses. If you plant weeds, you get weeds. Be very careful of the input of the world into your life. If you never read your Bible or talk to God but are letting the world input things into you heart and mind, you will not get good things out. Jesus said in Matthew 12:34b (TNIV), "Out of the overflow of the heart the mouth speaks." In other words, you get out what you put in.

So, did you recognize any of these things in your life? How is your location? Are you in a high traffic area and feel like you are being trampled? Has the soil eroded, or you feel like you weren't planted deep enough? Are you in a tiny pot and you feel comfortable there? We like to be in comfortable situations: change is hard, but if we want to grow, we must branch out and let our roots spread. We must not be a knot-head! Galatians 5:17 (TNIV) says this, "For the flesh desires what is contrary to the Spirit, and Spirit is contrary to the flesh. They conflict with each other, so that you are not to do whatever you want." You see, our sinful nature will not let us open ourselves up to the Spirit and we can't become beautiful because of it. However, if Jesus can have all of you, He can make you beautiful!

The last topic is about our roots. If you know anything about roots, I'm sure you know they carry food and water to the plant to keep it alive. If we don't have good spiritual roots we will die, just like those plants where the seeds fell on rocky soil. Plants need taproots. A taproot is the largest root on a plant and it goes the deepest into the ground, so that in time of drought the plant can still get water. It also stabilizes a plant, so it's not blown over in a storm or high wind. It's good for us to have a taproot that goes deep as well. We need the Holy Spirit to help us go deeper and deeper, so that when things happen, and they will, we will be firmly planted and able to receive the food and water to keep us alive.

You know there are lots of different flowers and plants. We all have a favorite. The next time you see a pretty flower, I want you to think about what it takes to make it grow to its potentially beautiful self. What does it need? Relate it to yourself and your spiritual life. Are you growing and healthy? Are you getting all the nutrients you need? Are you rooted in His Word so when a storm comes you stay strong? If you aren't, go to the Lord, He is always ready to tend His garden!

Headnotes

1   8BillionTrees.com, How Many Types of Flowers Are There? Identify flowers by Petal, Color and Zone, Written by Kim Williamson, March 30, 2023, Accessed June 13, 2023.

2   https://www.scu.edu.au>accc>plants of the garden Anemone(Lily of the Field, anemone coronara), Charles Sturt University-TEQSA Provider Identification: PRV 12018 (Australian University). CRICOS Provider: 5F. Accessed June 13, 2023.

CHAPTER 3

You are a Letter

Do you enjoy getting letters? Do you even get letters anymore? It seems like since technology has taken over our lives, that letters are almost a thing of the past! You may not get as many letters in the mail as you once did, but you are probably still getting some form of communication.

There are some letters that are very pleasant to get, like when you hear from someone who has been gone for awhile. Or perhaps you are receiving good news about a promotion, etc. There are also letters that are not so good, like Dear John letters, or bills! Some make us happy, some make us sad. Whatever the reason, they all have a purpose.

Let's look at what Scripture has to say. Second Corinthians 3:3 says, "You show that you are a letter from Christ, the result of our ministry, written not with ink but with the Spirit of the living God, not on tablets of stone, but on tablets of human hearts." This verse got me to thinking about what my being a letter from Christ might look like. Is my letter - AKA my life - showing other people what Jesus looks like? Am I being one of those good letters that people are happy about getting? Am I living so people see Jesus?

One way that we can live this life before others is found in the same verse we started with in this chapter. Second

Corinthians 3:3, "You show that you are a letter from Christ, written not with ink, but with the Spirit of the living God." Did you catch that? The Spirit of the living God!

God has given us His Spirit to help us live like He wants us to live. He's alive and well and has a purpose for every single one of us. If we are listening to His Spirit and allowing Him to show us the right way, we will be a wonderful letter to those around us.

Here are some verses that will help us understand how the Spirit of the living God works in our lives. First, let's look at John 16:13, "When the Spirit of truth, comes, he will guide you into all the truth, and he will not speak on his own, but only what he hears, and he will tell you what is yet to come." You see, the Spirit is hearing from God and He is guiding you so you can live pleasing to Him.

I enjoy being on tours guided by people who really know and have studied the area I'm touring. It makes things they tell me more authentic. Spiritually, it's wonderful to know we are being led through our life tour by the Spirit and we can be assured everything He tells us is true! That is very important these days. Truth is hard to come by. We don't have to worry about that with God!

Another verse that shows us how the Spirit helps us be a letter to others is John 14:26, "The Advocate, the Holy Spirit, whom the Father will send in my name, will teach you all things and will remind you of everything I have said to you." When the Holy Spirit is in our hearts, He is always teaching us and reminding us of what the Word of God says, so we can live the way Jesus wants us to.

Because we have all this help and more from His Spirit, we are able to have outward signs that will show others that we live Spirit controlled lives. Galatians 5:22-23, "But the fruit of the Spirit is love, joy, peace, forbearance (or patience), kindness, goodness, faithfulness, gentleness, and self-control. Against such things there is no law." Another great verse is Ephesians 4:32, "Be kind and compassionate to one another, forgiving each other, just as in Christ God forgave you."

I used to think that these things were in list form and that all I had to do was mark them off. I have to tell you, some of these things were easy for me, but some I am going to work on till Jesus comes back! That is where the Holy Spirit comes in with the guiding and teaching. We can't possibly do all these things or have all these things without Him!

You see, God is always working on our letters. He is showing the world what He looks like through us. Are we showing kindness, goodness, patience? Okay, patience is a hard one! But, seriously, can others see these fruits in our letter to them? I sure hope they can see at least some of them in me. I pray the Holy Spirit will keep working on me to help me in those areas where I'm lacking.

We've looked at what our letter from Christ looks like to others. Now, let's look at what that letter from Christ looks like to you. Just some questions first. How often do you hear from Jesus? What are some ways we get letters from Him? Are you putting yourself in a position to hear from Him? Has He asked you to do something? Remember, every letter has a purpose.

There are tons of ways for us to connect. I know I keep reiterating these things, but that's because they are important! First, read the Word. Get in there and find out what Jesus has to say. Here is where the Holy Spirit guides and teaches you, which is what we've been discussing.

One of the best things you can do is pray. Talk to Jesus. It doesn't have to be fancy. Just act like He is right there in the room with you because He is! Along with that, take the time to listen for answers. If you do, you'll be amazed at the things you hear! If you read my first book, "Power in Stillness", you know God asked me to write a book! Don't panic, He may not ask you to do that, but I guarantee you won't be disappointed with what He does ask you to do!

Some other ways you can get letters from God are through sermons. There are many ways this can be achieved: websites, YouTube, TV, blogs, and the list goes on. My goodness, everyone could hear the Word if they choose to do so.

Books are a great way to hear from the Lord as well. There are devotional books, entire books on different Biblical subjects, books on CD, podcasts, etc. Praise songs are wonderful ways to connect with the Spirit too. It doesn't matter if you like Southern Gospel, contemporary songs, or the hymns of the church, they are all full of words to connect you with Jesus.

You see, we all have numerous ways of hearing from God through his Holy Spirit. I'm sure glad He's given us so many ways to hear from Him. It helps me to know He's working on His end to get me where I need to be.

One last thing in Second Corinthians 3:3. There is a phrase that says, "The result of our ministry." I want you to think about this in two ways. First, whose ministry are you a result of? And second, who is the result of your ministry? Can you name people who have shaped you and led you through life? Can you name some people on which you have had an influence? I'm sure you can! If you ask God to give you a ministry, I'm certain He will. Let Him, through the Holy Spirit, guide you to someone who needs Him. There are a lot of people in the world who are hurting. You won't have trouble finding one and then another and another!

Let Jesus be the Author of the letter of your life. Give Him the opportunity to shine through you to others. He's just waiting.

Here is what Jesus' letter to you may sound like:

My Child,

I'm so glad you are mine! I have so many good things in store for you. I just need you to trust Me. Trust that I see the big picture. I see into the future and because I do, you can be assured that all is well. I love you so much. I *will* work all things together for your good. I know you are dealing with some hard stuff right now, but it's not the end! Since I'm in control and I know what is going to happen, You can trust that it's all going to work out. Trust My heart. Listen to My Spirit. Take time out to hear Me speak. Rest in the knowledge that I am taking care of you. Most of all, remember that I love you.

Your Friend,
Jesus

CHAPTER 4

Do You Smell Good?

What is your favorite smell? Is it food, perfume, or something else? One of my personal favorites is coffee. I also like to smell bread baking. Whatever that aroma may be, it can have the ability to transport your thoughts to another place, can't it? For instance, when I smell cigars, I think of the county fair when I was a kid. If I smell Old Spice, I remember my dad. Smells have that ability. What are some of your memories associated with a particular smell?

Did you know, "Women consistently score significantly higher than men on standard tests of smelling ability?"[1] I was going to say women smell better than men, or they smell more than men, but we all know neither of those is true! LOL.

Another thing about smell is how weak or strong they may be. I don't like to wear perfume that I smell all day. Seems like when I do that, I am almost sick by the end of the day. I just want to get a whiff of it every now and then. Have you ever been around someone drenched in a particular scent? UGH! If I can smell you coming, you are wearing too much!

There are good smells and there are bad smells. Think about the lovely odor of a skunk or a dead animal on the road. Yikes! Not so good. On the other hand, a beautiful rosebush or lilac has a wonderful aroma.

There were some fragrances talked about in the Bible too, and I want to give you a little background. We are going to use John 12:1-3 as our passage to begin. "Six days before the Passover, Jesus came to Bethany, where Lazarus lived, whom Jesus had raised from the dead. Here a dinner was given in Jesus' honor. Martha served, while Lazarus was among those reclining at the table with Him.

Then Mary took about a pint of pure nard, an expensive perfume: she poured it on Jesus' feet and wiped his feet with her hair. And the house was filled with the fragrance of the perfume."

That last phrase caught my attention. I got curious about this nard and decided to get a bit more information. Nard is also known as spikenard. It is an Asiatic plant that grows in the Himalaya's, India, and the far East. It was sealed in alabaster jars and imported. Nard was very expensive. Smith's Bible Dictionary says this: "The costliness of Mary's offering (300 pence + $45) may best be seen from the fact that a penny (denarius, 15-17 cents) was in those days the day wages of a laborer. (Matt. 20:2). In our day this would equal at least $300-$400 ED)."[2]

People used these oils to smell good because baths were few and far between. They also used the oils as protection from the sun. They were used for other purposes as well, such as preparing bodies for burial, for use as a medicine, to add to food, etc. As I was researching this, I found this article by Luisa Rodriguez in fruitfullyliving.com.: "There is an interesting correlation between the cross and how this oil is used today. Today, in hospice care, caregivers will use spikenard to help patients emotionally transition from life to death." When Mary anointed Jesus' feet, it was just a few days before

His crucifixion. I'm sure He was feeling the heaviness of death upon himself. Hopefully it helped relieve some of His stress! Spikenard was made from all parts of the plant, sometimes it was in oil form and sometimes in powder form or a sachet. There were times when this oil was so strong its aroma would last for centuries! Now we can understand why that fragrance filled the whole house!

Now, let's get down to relating this spiritually. First, we don't want to become nose blind! What in the world does that mean? You've probably seen the TV commercial about the kid who doesn't smell his room, but his mom comes in and wrinkles her nose. I have another example in mind as well. When my husband was in the army, we were stationed in Germany. We took a weekend tour bus and went to Paris, France, where one of our stops included a perfume factory. While on that tour, we learned that after smelling three samples, our ability to discern the difference in the fragrances didn't work anymore. That's why you might see coffee beans out at perfume counters. It helps clear your palate so you can discern smells again.

Okay, now let's equate this spiritually. We must be careful how many smells (sins) we allow to enter our arena! If we let one sin slide without asking God's forgiveness, then another and another may get through. Pretty soon we will be nose blind or sin blind, our spiritual nose will stop working. The further down this path we go, the worse off we become! Titus 1:15 in The Contemporary English Versions says: "Everything is pure for someone whose heart is pure. But nothing is pure for an unbeliever with a dirty mind. That person's mind and conscience are destroyed." You see, if we let too many things slide, in regard to sin, then our conscience is destroyed or obliterated. In Oswald Chambers Devotional, My Utmost for His Highest, he says this and it's so good!

"Conscience is that ability within me that attaches itself to the highest standard I know, and then continually reminds me of what that standard demands that I do. It is the eye of the soul which looks out either toward God or toward what we regard as the highest standard."[4] You see, we must make an effort to keep our conscience clean. When God speaks to us through our conscience about a particular area of our life that needs cleaning up, we need to listen to Him. Chambers also says, "The only thing that keeps our conscience sensitive to Him is the habit of being open to God on the inside. When you begin to debate, stop immediately. Don't ask, 'Why can't I do this?': You are on the wrong track. There is no debating possible once your conscience speaks. Whatever it is - drop it and see that you keep your inner vision clear."[5] We must be very careful to not become nose blind!

On to the next point. Did you know that God has a fragrance that He likes. He does! He wants us to smell like Jesus! Second Corinthians 2:15 says, "We are to God the aroma of Christ among those who are being saved and those who are perishing." God can identify us according to how we smell! Think about that in these terms. Can you identify someone by the way they smell? I've heard of people hugging the pillow of a loved one who passed away because they could still smell that special person on that pillow. Someone you know might wear a certain kind of perfume and you always think of that person when you smell it. According to the verse we just read, God knows who we are too, just because we smell like Jesus!

My next question is then, do we smell good or bad to other people? I sure hope we smell good, but the Bible says this in 2 Corinthians 2:16: "To the one we are an aroma that brings death: to the other, an aroma that brings life." We are not going to smell good as Christians to everyone. Why is that? The verse says we smell like death to the unsaved! You know that death is not a good smell at all. Even the tiniest animal can make a huge smell once it's passed away. I imagine people who don't know the Lord feel like we smell because their conscience doesn't like what they are doing. It makes them feel bad to know that they aren't living up to God's potential for them.

Even Jesus didn't smell good to some folks. Remember the Pharisees? They didn't like Him at all. As a matter of fact, they had Him put to death! Luke 2:34-35 says this about Jesus: "Then Simeon blessed them and said to Mary, his mother: 'This child is destined to cause the falling and rising of many in Israel, and to be a sign that is spoken against so that the thought and hearts of many will be revealed.'" John 3:36 tells us: "Whoever believes in the Son has eternal life, but whoever rejects the Son will not see life, for God's wrath remains on them." Personally, I would like to smell like life to people, even though I know there will be some who think I don't!

Which brings me to the next question: are we a lasting smell or do we dissipate quickly? Think back to the original verses of this chapter. The story where Mary was washing Jesus' feet, and the fragrance filled the house. Granted, back then the homes may not have been as large as some of our homes are today. But here is the point. Smells tend to waft from room to room. The aroma got to some people there before it reached others. John 12:9 tells us that there was a large crowd of Jews who had gathered there. They came not only to see Jesus, but also Lazarus, because remember he had been raised from the dead just a short time ago. So, when Mary broke that perfume jar and poured it out, the people at the front of the crowd smelled it first, then it drifted its way to the back of the crowd and filled the house! Here is my question to you, when you enter a house, is it filled with the fragrance of Jesus? Remember some of the oils lasted for centuries. We need to be a strong fragrance for Jesus. Not obnoxious, but sweet smelling! Do you have family and friends, children and grandchildren who could benefit from your smelling good? I hope you can say yes to that question!

Do you smell good?

Headnotes

1   The Smell Report-Sex Differences, SIRC, 53 Blandford Ave, Oxford, UK OX2, 1997-2020. http://www.sorc.org>smell_diffs

2   Smith, William, Dr. "Entry for Spikenard." Smith's Bible Dictionary…1901

3   Luisa Rodriguez, Mary of Bethany and an Essential Oil fit for a King!, June 25, 2017 Fruitfully Living Women, https://www.fruitfullyliving.

4   Chamber, Oswald. My Utmost for His Highest, edited by James Reimann. Discovery House Publishers, Box 3566 Grand Rapids, MI 49501 – May 13 insert

5   Ibid

CHAPTER 5

Jars of Clay

Second Corinthians 4:7-9 reads like this. "But we have this treasure in jars of clay to show that this all-surpassing power is from God and not from us. We are hard pressed, but not crushed, perplexed, but not in despair, persecuted, but not abandoned, struck down, but not destroyed."

Oh my, what great verses! There are a lot of things to find out about here. I want to start at the beginning and get some meaning to some of these phrases and words into our hearts.

The first phrase here says that we have this *treasure* in jars of clay. There are two things here we need to look at. The treasure spoken of here is the gospel, the good news about Jesus. Paul calls the gospel of Jesus a treasure because its value cannot be calculated. There is no way to gauge the cost of this good news. It changes lives and hearts, it cleanses us from sin, it guides and directs us. The gospel changes people from being in sin to living for Jesus! Goodness, who could put a price on that?

The second phrase we want to explore is *jars of clay*. I believe that Paul here is talking about our bodies. He understood that our bodies are fragile. We get sick, we get injured, our bodies get old and weak, then we die and move into a different phase of being. I know you've all heard the words, ashes to ashes, dust to dust. That is what happens to our bodies after death. They return to dust. So, in the very first part of this verse Paul is saying, we have this very priceless message of the gospel in this very fragile body, in a clay jar!

Back in Bible times, people would store their treasures in a clay vessel that had no beautiful outward appearance. That way no one who was looking for valuables would think to look there. Think about it this way. I've heard of people hiding money in a coffee can and putting it in the freezer! Who would think to look there?

The point of the first part about treasures in jars of clay is that we as Christians are imperfect. We may not be a perfect people (kind of like a coffee can), but inside we have this priceless treasure of Jesus! Because we are weak, Jesus can show the all-surpassing power of God. This is the next phrase in that sentence we need to look at. God has many ways to show His power. He is not limited by time or space. His omnipotence or all-powerful Being is best shown through us as his frail children. (Remember, jars of clay!)

What are some ways God shows His power? The next few parts of this verse will answer this question. Let's look at the first part. *We are hard-pressed, but not crushed.* The definition in **dictionary.com** says, "Hard-pressed means heavily burdened or oppressed."[1] I'm picturing someone who is broken. Do you know someone who is so beaten down that they can't see their way out? Are you that person? I want you to know the next phrase says, "but not crushed." Because of this gospel we're talking about, we don't have to stay in this crushed, broken state! Aren't you glad? Jesus came to give us life. John 14:6 is where Jesus said, He is the way, the truth, and the life. He also came to give us peace. In John 14:27 Jesus said, "Peace I leave with you; my peace I give you."

Jesus tells us over and over in His word not to be discouraged and not to be afraid. You see, we don't have to be crushed by all the things that press hard on us.

I could have quoted scripture after scripture promises that give us light and hope. Search for some of these on your own. I guarantee that God will meet you there and give you some special verses that fit your situation!

Alright, the next section we want to look at says *we are perplexed, but not in despair.* I thought I knew what perplexed and despair meant, but when I studied them a bit more, it goes deeper than I imagined.

The word perplexed, according to the Benson Commentary, says this, "It signifies persons involved in evils from which they know not how to extricate themselves."[2] In other words, they are in over their heads or in too deep! Ever been there? Ever been so uncertain that you don't know where to turn?

Sometimes these feeble bodies, our jars of clay, deceive us. They get us into this state of being perplexed. Notice the commentator said that it involved evils. When I think of Bible passages that demonstrate this, I think of King David. Remember how he got caught up in wanting and taking Bathsheba? He ended up having her husband murdered on the battlefield, then took her as his own wife. Do you think he was feeling perplexed, like there was no way out? Oh, you bet he was! He didn't know how to extricate himself from this evil, especially when his son was dying, but He was not in despair!

The definition of despair is to give up all hope of deliverance from God. David did not despair, he still had hope that God would forgive him. Guess what? God did forgive him, and He will forgive you too!

There is nothing too hard for God! There is no sin you've committed that He won't forgive! You only need to ask Him.

Next, the phrase *persecuted but not abandoned* is in our text. Persecuted means, "subject to hostility and ill treatment especially because of their ethnicity, religion, etc."[3] It also means to be harassed or opposed. The apostle Paul knew all about persecution from both sides. He was known and feared by a lot of Christians, because he had had many of them killed. Then Jesus met him on the road to Damascus and he became a Jesus follower. Because of this he was on the other side of the persecution fence. He says he was beaten, imprisoned, lashed with a whip, and pelted with stones, to name a few. (2 Corinthians 11:23-27). But he was not abandoned! He did not feel deserted or cast off. As a matter of fact, he says also in 2 Corinthians 12:10 "That is why, for Christ's sake, I delight in weaknesses, (jars of clay?) in insults, in hardships, in persecutions, in difficulties. For when I am weak, then I am strong." In my Bible where it says, "I delight," I have written, 'I am well content with'. See, Paul did not feel deserted or abandoned. He knew Who was with him no matter what he was going through. Do you? Are you letting God use His power to help you through things that happen in your life? I sure hope so.

Alright, on to the next part. *We are struck down, but not destroyed.* When I went to gotquestions.org and asked what struck down meant, it said, "portrays something getting hit, abused, abandoned, or even killed."[4] So, it is similar to being persecuted, but doesn't necessarily have the element of ethnicity or religion involved. Many, many people live in abusive situations. There are a lot of children living in homes that are bad for their health. Some little ones are abandoned and left with relatives or complete strangers. But the apostle

Paul says we are not destroyed. We get knocked around by life, some of us worse than others. But God in His wisdom doesn't leave us there.

As I was thinking about this, a toy from a while back came to mind. Do you remember Weeble Wobbles? You probably remember the commercial for it said, "Weebles wobble, but they don't fall down!" You could try your hardest to knock one of these things over, but they just keep righting themselves! It's the same way with us, only we have Jesus to help bring us back up! We are not destroyed if we keep our eyes on Him!

Sometimes we as Christians go through hard times. We may be perplexed, hard-pressed, persecuted or struck down, BUT… we have this all- surpassing power from God to help us keep going! He will not leave you crushed or broken; he will not leave you in despair or abandoned. You will not be destroyed. Because of His power you can trust Him, He is your Hope. Yes, you are embodied in a jar of clay, but God understands you and is working to help you through the next phase of your journey here on Earth. Stay strong in His Spirit and seek Him everyday!

Headnotes

1   Dictionary.com, s.v. "hard-pressed," accessed July 11, 2023, https://www.dictionary.com

2   Benson Commentary, "perplexed", accessed July 11, 2023, https://www.biblehub.com

3   Oxford English Dictionary, s.v. "persecuted," accessed July 11, 2023, https://www.oed.com

4   "What does struck down mean?" Got Questions Ministries, accessed July 11, 2023, [https://www.gotquestions.org/what-is-struck-down.html]

CHAPTER 6

Are You a Little Salty?

When our family lived in Germany while my husband was stationed there, we took a trip to a salt mine. It's been a minute or two since then, but I remember most the dark tunnels back into a mountain. I also remember riding a slide down to a lower level on a piece of leather. That was certainly an exciting trip! Since that time, I haven't thought a lot about salt, except that I like to use it as a seasoning. However, I did a study on it because I came across the word several times in my Bible reading.

Salt really is kind of interesting when you start looking into it. Of course, we all know that today it is used as a condiment or seasoning. It was used in the past in the same way. Additionally, salt was used to preserve food. Animals also used it. Today, farmers put out salt licks for their cattle because their bodies need a certain amount of it.

Salt comes in different colors like pink, red, white, yellow, and even green and red! The color differences are caused by different minerals. The darker the salt, the more minerals it has in it.

It was used as a preservative in historical times as I mentioned before, and we still use it that way today. We use it in beef jerky, pickles, and canned goods because it keeps microbes from growing by reducing the water activity in food.

Medicine was and is now, another use for salt. In the past, babies were bathed in salt water, then rubbed with salt when they were born to ward off any infection. People use saltwater to gargle for sore throats. It's good for nasal passages too. Saline solution is used for surgeries, in dentistry and IV solutions. There are lots of different medical uses beyond those listed here.

"In ancient Rome, soldier's pay was known as 'solarium argentum'. This is where we get our word salary. Part of a soldier's pay was paid in salt. If a soldier's salary was cut, he was said to, 'not be worth his salt.' The busiest road in Rome was called 'Via Salaria,' or the salt route. Romans and Greeks often bought slaves with salt."[1]

It sure seems like salt has an interesting history in our world. There were several times in our Bible that salt was mentioned too. We will start with some of the Old Testament citations, then move to the New. I'm going to try to help you understand how these things apply to us today as Christians living in our world and why it's so important.

Let's get started with Leviticus 2:13, "Season all of your grain offering, with salt. Do not leave the salt of the covenant of your God out of your grain offerings; add salt to all your offerings." The King James Version also includes meat in this verse. Ellicott's Commentary for English Readers says, "In the east when people eat bread and salt together it means there is a mutual amity, or friendly relationship. When Arabs make a covenant together, they put salt on the blade of a sword from whence everyone puts a little into his mouth. This consti-tutes them blood relations, and they remain faithful to each other even when in danger of life." (Ritter, Erd.14:960).[2] So, a covenant of salt is an alliance or everlasting covenant. You see, God wanted, first for the Levites to be taken care of physically, by providing all their food and other needs. He also wanted them to know that He was going to carry on this unbreakable pact He had with them. He was going to take care of them always, with a covenant of salt!

Isn't that exactly what He does for us too? He works in our everyday lives to keep us and sustain us and help us to live for Him. Once we've accepted Him, the covenant is there and in place. He is going to take care of us. He made a covenant with us, not with salt, but with the blood of Jesus. I love that! God is so good!

Another place in the Old Testament that speaks of salt is the famous passage about Lot's wife. If you are familiar with the story, you know it's in Genesis 19. Lot and his family were told they needed to leave Sodom because God was going to destroy it! It took a little convincing, but finally they were on their way. The two angels told them to flee and not look back and don't stop. By the time Lot and his family got to Zoar the sun had come up and God overthrew the cities of Sodom and Gomorrah. Two verses after that, a very sad statement is made. Verse 26 says, "Lot's wife looked back, and she became a pillar of salt." Wow! Some commentators think it's possible that she may have been longing to look back at what she was leaving behind or maybe her curiosity got the better of her. They think that she may have been close enough to the fire and brimstone that she was caught in it and turned to salt. If she had kept going, she would have been okay. Is there a lesson here for us? I think there is! Once Jesus saves us, we should never look back or yearn for things from our past. We need to be obedient to Him and move forward and do what He tells us. We need to get it into our hearts and our heads where our real treasure lies. Matthew 6:20-21 says, "But store up for yourselves treasures in heaven, where moths and vermin do not destroy, and where thieves do not break in and steal. For where your treasure is, there your heart will be also."

Alright, moving on to the New Testament. Let's look at some places where salt is mentioned. In Matthew 5:13 Jesus tells us, "You are the salt of the earth. But if the salt loses its saltiness, how can it be made salty again? It is no longer good for anything, except to be thrown out and trampled underfoot!" As I was studying this, I found that the priests in the Temple would throw out salt that was worthless onto the floor of the Temple so that it wasn't slick. It was also used for walking paths because wherever it was put down, nothing would grow! So, no slipping and no weeds!

Another thing I found that was interesting was that in the Valley of Salt, if you were to break a piece off a salt rock, it would lose its flavor. It might still sparkle, but it would have no taste. The connected part would still retain its flavor. This reminds me of what happens to us if we don't stay connected to Jesus and the church! We will not retain joy and grace and forgiveness if we don't stay in touch with Him.

Colossians 4:5-6 is another set of verses about salt. "Be wise in the way you act toward outsiders; make the most of every opportunity. Let your conversation be always full of grace, seasoned with salt, so that you may know how to answer everyone." Notice how Paul here gives us directions on how to deal with other people. He tells us to be wise and gracious and seasoned with salt. I think that means we need to be listening to the Holy Spirit and speak what we need to speak, but also to be quiet when we need to be quiet. Too much salt will make a dish inedible. Pushing too much will only make a person turn away. If we will only tune in to what God is speaking, we can say just the right thing at just the right time and help someone find Jesus or help them through a problem!

James 3:9-12 also gives us some instruction on how to deal with others and uses the word salt! "With the tongue we praise our Lord and Father, and with it we curse human beings, who have been made in God's likeness. Out of the same mouth come praise and cursing. My brothers and sisters, this should not be. Can both fresh water and saltwater flow from the same spring? My brothers and sisters, can a fig tree bear olives, or a grapevine bear figs? Neither can a salt spring produce fresh water." I saw a picture one time of a place in the Gulf of Alaska where fresh water and saltwater come together. The cool thing is that there is a definite line where they meet. They will not mix because fresh water is less dense than salt water. So, what is James really saying? If you truly have the Holy Spirit in you and guiding you, then the things you say should be uplifting and beneficial. If, however, your heart is not in the right place and you are saying things that are not right or helpful, there is a problem. You see, the two cannot mix, just like fresh and salt water. The other parts of that verse say you don't get figs off an olive tree. It's the same concept!

Along that same line, in Luke 6:45 Jesus said, "Good people bring good things out of the good stored up in their heart and evil people bring evil things out of the evil in their heart. For out of the overflow of the heart the mouth speaks." What is in our hearts tends to come out of our mouths. Oh, Lord, I need help!

I hope you have been able to see some things in this lesson that will help you. If all you learned was facts about salt, then I didn't do my job. I pray that you will see the important parts that Scripture brings to us and that you will be able to use it in your everyday life. How we treat others, by the words we use, comes from within us. Salt can be a good thing if it hasn't lost its flavor. I hope you haven't lost your flavor. If you feel like you have, go to Jesus, and let Him restore you. He will do that very thing!

Headnotes

1   Time Staff, "A Brief History of Salt," Time, March 15, 1982, https://time.com/395760/a-brief- history-of-salt/

2   Ellicot's Commentary for English Readers. https://biblehub.com/commentaries/ellicott.   (Ritter, Erd.14:960)

CHAPTER 7

Shields - God as our Protector

Do you ever feel like you need protection? In this day and age, I think we all feel a bit of trepidation. All we have to do is turn on the television, pick up our phone or get on our computer. It won't take long to figure out that our world can be scary!

One day as I was reading my Bible, I came across the word shield several times. It seems that God uses topics a lot of times to catch my attention. I wrote this lesson on shields because of that, so let's get into it!

You may be like me and need just a little background or history on shields, as this is not something I know much about. First, there were several materials used to make shields and some of that was dependent on the time period in which they were used! Some were made from leather, some from bronze. Others were made of brass, wood, gold or even wicker. (Not sure how much protection that was! Maybe if you were fighting with feathers!)

There were also different shapes used and sizes as well. Some were made to cover the entire body and a soldier could stick it in the ground and then stand behind it to shoot. Some were small and round and held on one arm, while the soldier used the other arm for his sword.

Some shields were made for hand-to-hand combat while others were used on horseback. In the story of David and Goliath, a shield used by Goliath's attendant covered his entire body. It must have been huge when you think that he and Goliath came from a race of giants! The reference for that story is 1 Samuel 17:7, 14.

I wanted to give you an idea how shields were made, but I also wanted you to be aware of how they were used. Not only were the small ones used on the arm, but I saw a movie once showing a group of soldiers with long, tall shields. These guys formed rows with the first row putting their shields down in front with the man kneeling behind. The next row came behind the kneeling soldier and put his shield over his head. The next row did the same, etc. Now, picture what I'm describing, the first two rows look like an upside down L. Then with the rest of the rows behind them, they were making a crude, but effective shelter of sorts. I thought that was pretty ingenious!

We actually have shields today too, but unless you are military or police, you may not think much about it. You know we have windshields on our cars and motorcycles (thank goodness or we'd be eating bugs!) Thankfully, we are not doing much hand to hand combat anymore. Whatever the type of shield or the time period it was used in, the reason was pretty much the same. Someone needed protection.

God has given us some great promises in His Word about He Himself being our shield or our protector. Let's look at some of His Words of encouragement.

Here are three verses that will help us live in this world. The first verse we want to look at is Genesis 15:1. This is the first time shields are mentioned in the Bible. "After this, the word of the LORD came to Abram in a vision: 'Do not be afraid, Abram, I am your shield, your very great reward.'"

Think about what that verse is saying. God was telling Abram that He was Abram's protector! And not only that, He was also Abram's great reward! When we have found God, we've certainly found a great reward. We have found a treasure! If we have a personal relationship with God, we have the ability to be in contact with Him. I think it's interesting that God tells Abram, not to be afraid. Just like your children are not afraid when they feel protected or shielded by you! If there was a riot going on, would you be more afraid in front of the line of guys with shields, or behind them? See, God is always out in front of us, protecting us, keeping us safe. We have nothing to fear! Our reward is a fresh, daily renewing of our souls, along with a lot of other blessings.

The next scripture we want to look at is 2 Samuel 22:3 (TNIV). King David actually sang these words to the Lord after God had saved him from King Saul. This is also found in Psalm 18. Here's what he sang, "The LORD is my rock, my fortress, and my deliverer; my God is my rock, in whom I take refuge, my shield and the horn of my salvation. He is my stronghold, my refuge and my savior - from violent people you save me." Can you tell that David thought God was protecting him? Again, God was helping him get through every day! If you continue reading in that chapter, you will see the imagery used there is amazing. God's protection and help for him was powerful, as powerful as lightning and thunder or an earthquake. That's the way I want to be protected!

I also want to tell you about that phrase, *my shield and the horn of my salvation*. This comes from when the Temple was built in the Old Testament. "The horns were used to indicate the corners of the altar. The horns and the altar were to be made of the same wood. The brass overlay was required so that the horn could endure the fire and preserve the wood from destruction. Our bodies are represented by the wood, and Christ's blood is the brass overlay, which brightens and protects us from divine wrath."[1] Can you see the shield here? The brass shielded the wood and Jesus shields us! Just amazing!

The next verse is still in 2 Samuel 22. Let's check out verse 36. The NKJV says: "You have also given me the shield of Your salvation: Your gentleness hath made me great." The NIV 1984 ed. Says: "You give me your shield of victory and your right hand sustains me; you stoop down to make me great." What does *you give me your shield of victory* mean, if not that He is helping us be successful! I love that! God doesn't want us to fail. The next part of that verse speaks of sustaining us as well. He's keeping us, and working with us, giving us direction.

Another cool thing to look at in that verse is the last part about God stooping down and if we look at the NKJV it says gentleness. If we combine those two, I get this mental picture of a Daddy with his little toddler. The child may have fallen or is trying to accomplish some task, and the Dad gets on his knees, or stoops to help that little one. Can you see it? Can you picture God stooping down in His gentleness helping you to fix that problem? Helping you live for him? Helping you through each day? Wow! What a great verse! He's already given us the win! That's what Jesus accomplished on the cross!

The next verse we need to look at is Psalm 28:7a. (BSB) "The LORD is my strength and my shield; my heart trusts in Him and I am helped." Sometimes, I feel like I need a little round shield, but there are other times I feel like I need a huge body shield! Kind of like the one Goliath's armor bearer used! I know you've been there! When you go through a really rough time like the death of a loved one, divorce, a job loss, or any number of other hard times, it's good to know that God is our shield and strength. When we trust Him, we are helped.

In Psalm 7:10 it says "My shield is God Most High, who saves the upright in heart." In the footnotes it uses the word sovereign for the word shield. A sovereign is a ruler or king. Now, think about this; your King is God Most High. He will save you. Isn't that usually what a king does? Don't they usually protect their subjects? At least that's what they are supposed to do, and our God does an awesome job of that!

Okay, on to Psalm 91:4: "He will cover you with His feathers, and under His wings you will find refuge; his faithfulness will be your shield and rampart." Again, we find God protecting us like a mother bird protects her babies. To me the word faithfulness means loyal and steadfast. I'm so glad God has stayed loyal to me over my lifetime. He has blessed me and protected me during some rough times. He was truly my shield when our daughter passed away suddenly in a car accident. God just kept bringing me words of grace, peace, and hope. If He hadn't been there every step of the way, I would probably be lost, and you wouldn't be reading these words. He is real. He protects us when we can't protect ourselves. I'm so thankful!

One last verse, although I could cite many more. Ephesians 6:16 tells us, "In addition to all this, take up the shield of faith, with which you can extinguish all the flaming arrows of the evil one." All the other verses we looked at were about God being our shield and protector and place of refuge. This verse, however, says *we* need to do something. *We* must pick up our shield of faith in Jesus. Notice it says to extinguish the flaming arrows. Satan will throw all kinds of things at you. The only way to combat him is to have your shield ready. Soldiers used to soak their leather shields in water to help put out the flaming arrows. Jesus is the Living

Water, so we need Him to be our shield to help extinguish the arrows thrown at us. What is that shield? Jesus and His Word. Get the Word in your heart and your mind. Hear His Voice and let Him speak peace to your soul!

So, what am I really saying here? Don't leave home without this vital piece of your armor! You need Jesus to go before you. Soak up all of Him that you can possibly hold. Then when you need protection or you are fighting the enemy, you will be prepared and be victorious!

In our day, we aren't as familiar with shields as they may have been in Bible times, but I'm here to tell you, I'm sure glad that God is still in the protecting and shielding business. He always knows exactly the type of shield we need, and He employs it at the first sign of battle!

Headnotes

1   Napier, Chad. https://www.Christianity.com What does the Horn of Salvation Mean? Accessed July 3, 2023, Copyright 2023.

CHAPTER 8

Oh, Those Dry Bones!

Picture this! You are in the desert and you are speaking to the Spirit of God. There are dry bones lying everywhere. The sun is beating down and you can tell from looking at those bones that they have been there for a long, long time. There is no longer any skin on those bones. They are lying haphazardly on the ground. Can you imagine walking through those bones and hearing them brush up against each other? Can you imagine the sound they would make? This is where the prophet Ezekiel found himself in the passage of scripture we are going to look at in this lesson.

Here is the passage of Ezekiel 37:1-14:

"The hand of the LORD was on me, and he brought me out by the Spirit of the LORD and set me in the middle of a valley; it was full of bones. He led me back and forth among them, and I saw a great many bones on the floor of the valley, bones that were very dry. He asked me, "Son of man, can these bones live?"

I said, "Sovereign LORD, you alone know."

Then he said to me, "Prophesy to these bones and say to them, 'Dry bones, hear the word of the LORD! This is what the Sovereign LORD says to these bones: I will make breath enter you, and you will come to life. I will attach tendons to you and make flesh come upon you and cover you with skin; I will put breath in you, and you will come to life. Then you will know that I am the LORD.'"

So I prophesied as I was commanded. And as I was prophesying, there was a noise, a rattling sound, and the bones came together, bone to bone. I looked, and tendons and flesh appeared on them, and skin covered them, but there was no breath in them.

Then he said to me, "Prophesy to the breath; prophesy, son of man, and say to it, 'This is what the Sovereign LORD says: Come, breath, from the four winds and breathe into these slain, that they may live.'" So I prophesied as he commanded me, and breath entered them; they came to life and stood up on their feet—a vast army.

Then he said to me: "Son of man, these bones are the people of Israel. They say, 'Our bones are dried up and our hope is gone; we are cut off.' Therefore prophesy and say to them: 'This is what the Sovereign LORD says: My people, I am going to open your graves and bring you up from them; I will bring you back to the land of Israel. Then you, my people, will know that I am the LORD, when I open your graves and bring you up from them. I will put my Spirit in you, and you will live, and I will settle you in your own land. Then you will know that I the LORD have spoken, and I have done it, declares the LORD.'"

I imagine that was quite a trip for Ezekiel! He was transported in his mind, or we would call it a vision, to this valley filled with dry bones. The Spirit of God then asked him if these bones could live again. Ezekiel was wise in answering that only God would know the answer to that.

Then the Spirit told him to prophecy. As I investigated the word prophecy, I found that it means to speak on God's behalf, at least in this passage. Here is what He had to say through Ezekiel, "Dry bones, hear the word of the LORD! I will make breath enter you, and you will come to life. I will attach tendons to you and make flesh come upon you and cover you with skin. I will put breath in you and you will come to life. Then you will know that I am the LORD."

Several things stand out to me here. First, the bones were made into bodies, but the bodies couldn't/didn't breathe until Ezekiel prophesied. Think about this. Before we are saved by Jesus we are as dead spiritually as those bones with skin on them. We are walking around, but we have no life! Did you feel like that before you came to Jesus? Do you feel like that right now? Something to think about.

I think it's interesting that there was no life in those bones and flesh until God breathed on them. Here is what the Lord said to him. "Prophesy to the breath; prophesy, son of man, and say to it, 'This is what the Sovereign LORD says: Come, breath, from the four winds and breathe into these slain, that they may live.'" So I prophesied as he commanded me, and breath entered them; they came to life and stood up on their feet—a vast army." Until that time they were just bodies, but not really alive! Isn't that the way it is for us too? We aren't really alive till Jesus comes and breathes His Spirit into us. We need God's grace to open up our heart, eyes and ears to be able to know Him. Prevenient grace is so important. What that means is that God is working in your heart and mind bringing you to Him, before (that is the "pre" part of that word) you even know that you need Him. It is so important for we who are Christians to pray for this in other's lives. Ask the Holy Spirit to meet with and draw that unsaved person or persons in your life to Himself. That is what we are talking about here.

The third thing that comes to mind is where God says to the bones, "Hear the Word of the LORD." We don't really come alive until we hear from Him and the way we hear from Him is through His Word. The Bible is such an awesome book. It covers so many of our questions. It gives us direction, comfort, peace, shows us Jesus, helps us know how to live for Him, and so much more. My question to you is, are you listening? Are you reading His Word? Do you spend time with Him, asking and seeking and diligently trying to find Him?

Without the Spirit helping us breathe we will not get to the end result, the saving of our souls. Let's look at what the end of this passage says. [13]"Then you, my people, will know that I am the LORD, when I open your graves and bring you up from them. [14]I will put my Spirit in you, and you will live, and I will settle you in your own land. Then you will know that I the LORD have spoken, and I have done it, declares the LORD.'" Do you see all the promises there? Oh, my goodness!

First, we will know that He is God! 1 Corinthians 2:12-16 says it well, [12]"What we have received is not the spirit of the world, but the Spirit who is from God, so that we may understand what God has freely given us. [13]This is what we speak, not in words taught us by human wisdom but in words taught by the Spirit, explaining spiritual realities with Spirit-taught words. [14]The person without the Spirit does not accept the things that come from the Spirit of God but considers them foolishness, and cannot understand them because they are discerned only through the Spirit. [15]The person with the Spirit makes judgments about all things, but such a person is not subject to merely human judgments, [16]for, 'Who has known the mind of the Lord so as to instruct him?' But we have the mind of Christ." You see, once you have the Spirit of God living and breathing in you, you will be able to understand what the Word of God means!

Second, when He gives us His Spirit, we will be alive! Not just physically, but emotionally, and spiritually. He will open those graves! Yeah! So exciting!

Third, He will settle us in our own land. What? What does that mean? I think it may mean that we will have peace in our hearts. In this passage God was giving the Israelites a home, a place to call their own, where they could be safe and worship Him. Doesn't He do that for us too? He gives us peace to settle us down so we can serve Him and worship Him alone. I love that!

Last, in that fourteenth verse it says we will know that it was God who did all this for us. "Then you will know that I the LORD have spoken, and I have done it, declares the LORD!" He does great things for us all the time. In this passage He gave the Israelites life, and breath and peace and He will do the same things for us, if we will listen closely to what is being said.

Well, hallelujah! God has done great things! He makes dry bones come together by putting tendon, muscle, and skin on them. But those bones wouldn't have come alive without God breathing on them. Has He breathed on you yet? I sure hope so. If He has, ask Him to breathe on someone else you know so that His prevenient grace can go to work! They need you. They need His Holy Spirit!

CHAPTER 9

The Storm is Raging

Do you have any storms raging in your life right now? I hope not, but I wouldn't be surprised if you do! It's okay, you know, if you do have a storm happening. We are going to look at what we can do if we encounter a storm in our lives and have some ways to deal with them.

Mark 4:35-41 and Matthew 8:23-27 are basically the same stories. They tell about Jesus calming a physical storm in the lives of the disciples, and we will study that in a bit, but I want to also look at storms in your life today.

The Mark version of this story is given here.

"That day when evening came, he said to his disciples, "Let us go over to the other side." Leaving the crowd behind, they took him along, just as he was, in the boat. There were also other boats with him. A furious squall came up, and the waves broke over the boat, so that it was nearly swamped. Jesus was in the stern, sleeping on a cushion. The disciples woke him and said to him, "Teacher, don't you care if we drown?"

He got up, rebuked the wind, and said to the waves, "Quiet! Be still!" Then the wind died down and it was completely calm.

He said to his disciples, "Why are you so afraid? Do you still have no faith?"

They were terrified and asked each other, "Who is this? Even the wind and the waves obey him!"

Let's think about the storm for a minute. The disciples were in the boat and the storm came up quickly. They were scared and worried that they would go down with the waves that were crashing over the edge of their boat. They cried out to Jesus who was asleep! He got up and told the wind to settle down, and it does, to the amazement of the men on board with him. That must have been pretty scary!

Guess what? You have had scary things come up quickly in your lives too. I know you have. I know, because you are human. Jesus himself told us we would have troubles happen in life. If you haven't yet had any troubles, then just hold on a bit, because you certainly will at some point!

We sometimes call these storms, hard times or trials. Whatever you want to call them, they are NOT nice! They are frightening and can come so quickly that we are left feeling like we are drowning. I'm going to sound like I'm veering off subject here just a bit, but I will bring it all together for you.

When I taught elementary school my favorite subject was science. One of the things I had to teach was about rocks. Metamorphic rocks are "formed when rocks are subjected to heat, high pressure, hot mineral fluids or a combination of these things."[1] What all that heat and pressure does for rocks is make them really hard and tough!

Oh, no! You are saying to yourself about now, she's going to say this trial or storm I'm going through is making me tough! I don't want to be tough! The problem is, we don't have much choice, do we? Unfortunately, STUFF HAPPENS! I heard this saying at a conference once, "A stream with no rocks makes no music!" Think about that a minute. If the water is smooth and flowing with nothing to break it up, it doesn't make any sound. However, there is nothing like the sound of a creek that has some rocks in it. I think I could even go to sleep listening to that sound! Of course, that isn't what usually happens when we encounter rocks/problems is it?

So, here is where I'm coming back to our storm and how to get help for it. There are three ways that have been identified to categorize stressful situations, freeze, fight, and flight.

When a person is in freeze mode they are paralyzed, overwhelmed, or hyper-vigilant. Think of deer in the headlights! I hate watching a movie when they show a car going through an intersection and in the background we, the audience, can see another vehicle coming at the one in the intersection. You just know what is about to happen and you want to yell at them to move! But they are frozen in time.

The second response to stress is fight mode. In this response a person might feel a sense of aggression or even self-defense. When I find myself in this mode, I tend to blame someone else for something, instead of taking the responsibility for myself. The sense of aggression is also something prevalent in our world today. There are lots of folks with anger issues. Maybe stress is the trigger? This causes many issues at work or in our family life if we let this anger fester.

The third and final response mode is flight. In this mode a person would seek to escape or avoid the problem. I think they feel like if they can just get away from the problem, maybe it will go away. Guess what? When you do that, your problem goes with you! So, what are we to do then?

Before we go on to answer that, I'd like you to think back to the Bible story at the beginning of this chapter. Which of these three things, freeze, fight, or fight, was how the disciples handled this stress? I believe that they had at least two of these things.

First, I think they were in freeze mode. They were overwhelmed when we hear them saying, "Lord, save us, we are going to drown!" Isn't freeze mode really fear? Sometimes, the way we feel isn't always logical, is it?

Second, I think the disciples were in fight mode as well. Remember the questions, "Teacher, don't you care if we drown? Do you think they were a little on the defensive here? Maybe just a tad bit of aggression showing through. Have you ever felt that way toward circumstances or even toward God? You know, why me Lord? I think we have all been there at some point in our lives.

I also think that God is offering us another way to handle that stress and here is where the meat of the lesson comes in. When your circumstances are overwhelming just S-T-O-P! If you remember, I talked about this in the first chapter. Now I will explain a bit more about it.

First, S= Seek God! The first thing the disciples did was wake Jesus up! Remember where He was? He was asleep in the boat! The disciples knew Who to go to for help! I think that is a good model for us as well. Deuteronomy 4:29 says this, "But *if* from there you *seek* the LORD your God, you *will* find him *if* you *seek* him with all your heart and with all your soul." Think about those disciples; do you think they were calm, cool, and collected when they went to wake Jesus up? I'm pretty sure they knew exactly WHO they were seeking! They knew Jesus was the only ONE who was going to help them get out of this situation.

Second Chronicles 15:2b says, "The LORD is with you when you are with him. If you *seek* him, he *will* be found by you, but if you forsake him, he will forsake you." Notice all those italicized words there. I did that on purpose. I want you to realize that *if* you *seek* Him, you *will* find Him. It is a promise from God to you!

Jeremiah 29:12-14 is another set of verses saying," Then you will call on me and come and pray to me, and I *will* listen to you. You *will seek* me and *find* me when you *seek* me with all your heart. I *will* be found by you," declares the LORD, "and *will* bring you back from captivity." Every one of these verses tells us that He will be found by us if we are seeking Him diligently. I love that!

I want to give you an illustration from science again. Do you know anything about mixtures and solutions? A mixture is something that can be taken apart. For instance, think of a tossed salad. If you were of a mind too, you could sit and take apart all the pieces of that salad and put them in piles according to what they are: lettuce pieces with lettuce, onion with onion, etc.

A solution on the other hand is when something is dissolved in a liquid. For example, salt water. The salt is mixed up in that water until you can't see it anymore. The only way to separate it would be to let all the water evaporate from it and then you would have salt again. Here is my analogy. If we are seeking God, He is as available to us as that water was to the salt. He will be involved in every problem we have, and we won't want to be anywhere else because we have Him as our source of help! He can be in every conversation, every problem, every moment of every day *if* we let Him.

The next letter we want to look at is T. The T stands for trust His heart! Do you think the disciples in the boat with Jesus trusted Him? I think they did. I'm not sure exactly what they thought He was going to do, but they knew He would do something to help them. Does your fear trump your trust in Jesus? I hope not, but sometimes in the midst of that storm, it gets kind of hard!

Psalm 9:10 says,

"Those who know your name *trust* in you, for you, LORD, have never forsaken those who seek you." Psalm 18:2, "The LORD is my rock, my fortress and my deliverer, my God is my rock, in whom I take refuge, my shield and the horn of my salvation, my stronghold." Oh my, I could do another lesson on just that verse! Isaiah 26:3-4, "You will keep in perfect peace those whose minds are steadfast, because they *trust* in you. Trust in the LORD forever, for the LORD, the LORD himself is the Rock eternal."

There is a song by Babbie Mason titled Trust His Heart. Here are the words to the chorus:

"God is too wise to be mistaken

God is too good to be unkind

So when you don't understand

When you don't see His plan

When you can't trace His hand

Trust His heart."[2]

One last thing about trust: This is a quote from Sarah Young in Jesus Lives, "When you are afraid, don't blame yourself for having that very human emotion. Instead acknowledge it, then affirm your trust in Jesus-out loud or in a whisper. This protects you from the lie that feeling fear means you don't trust Him."[3]

On to the next step. O=Obey what He tells you to do! Read His Word! Listen for His Voice, follow His commands.

Think about our story of the disciples in the storm. They watched as the wind and waves obeyed Jesus! That must have been quite a sight!

Psalm 119:9-16 is a great passage of Scripture. It tells us how young people can keep their way pure. Listen to this: How can those who are young keep their way pure? By *living* according to your word. I *seek* you with all my heart: do not let me stray from your commands. I have *hidden your word* in my heart that I might not sin against you. Praise be to you, LORD; *teach* me your decrees. With my lips I *recount* all the laws that come from your mouth. I *rejoice* in following your statutes as one rejoices in great riches. I *meditate* on your precepts and consider your ways. I *delight* in your decrees; I will *not neglect* your word." Again, notice the words in italics. They point out to you the things you can do to obey the Lord and live for him. It doesn't just apply to young people; it can apply to you no matter your age!

And that leads us to the P in STOP. P=Perseverance. Persevere means, "to continue in a course of action even in the face of difficulty or with little or no prospect of success." Do you think the disciples in our story persevered? Have you read the New Testament? Long after Jesus saved them in that boat that day, they certainly persevered! Most of them till the day they were martyred.

We too must hang in there! Perseverance is hard work! It is keeping on when you can't see any way it could possibly work out. This is a cool place to be because the next thing that can happen is probably going to be a miracle. Sometimes life becomes overwhelming. I am amazed sometimes at what God has brought me through. I am amazed at stories you have that God has brought you through. Some of you are living through some things right now that are incredibly overwhelming. Can I say, please don't give up? We must keep going!

If you have sought God, trusted Him to give you the answer, been obedient, then you must persevere. Continue with these things till Jesus answers your prayer. I'm so thankful we have the Holy Spirit to help us with this. We couldn't make it without Him.

God has brought me through several storms. I guarantee He has done the same for you! Are we tougher because of it? I know we are.

Give those problems to Jesus and let him handle them. STOP. Seek Him. Trust His Heart. Obey what He tells you to do. Persevere. Let Him take care of it for you!

Headnotes:

1   U.S. Department of the Interior. Metamorphic Rock. Accessed August 22, 2022. https://www.usgs.gov.

2   Mason, Babbie. "Trust His Heart." Essential Music Publishing, 2001, Accessed April 15, 2023, https://music.youtube.com

3   Young, Sarah. Jesus Lives. Nashville, Tennessee: Thomas Nelson, 2009. P. 164.

CHAPTER 10

Glimpses of God

How does God surprise you? Have you gotten any surprises from Him lately? I sure hope you have because when God shows up in unexpected ways it's pretty awesome! I've been made aware recently that there are things in my life that God is taking care of for me and I wasn't even aware that there was a need! However, God knew, and had it all worked out before I realized what was going on! Isn't that just like God? Looking out for us even when we don't know we need to be looked out for! I love that!

Here is an example that happened just recently. My daughter and family went on vacation, so my husband and I were taking care of their place. They have goats and chickens, and some other animals too. I went out because one of the baby goats got his head stuck through the fence. I was able to get him unstuck, checked to see that they had water and noticed that the gate to the pen was open! OH, NO! I wasn't even sure how many goats they have, so, I'm just getting ready to text my daughter when I get a text from her. She's telling me that the goats are out! She has a way of seeing their pen on her phone, so she was a little freaked out too!

I called her and asked how many goats they had. She told me 12. When I told her they were all there, she asked if it was raining. It just so happened that it was raining very lightly. You see, the goats don't like rain, so they headed back to their shelter right before I got back there. I didn't see one goat out and chased exactly zero goats, because it rained just enough to shoo them back in! I said all that to say this, I believe God was watching out for me that day, even though I wasn't even aware that I needed it till after the fact! What a good, good Father He is to take care of the goats for me. I love it!

Now, some may think that is coincidence, but I want you to know that we hadn't had any rain for a long time. God knew just what was needed to get those crazy goats back where they needed to be. My daughter told me later that she had no idea how in the world I would ever get them back in their pen. She says they are hard to wrangle, but you know what? Rain from God did the trick!

Another example is from our Pastor and his wife. They had ordered a small piece of furniture online and it came in a weird sized box. They got it out and put it together, then realized it wasn't what they had ordered. This of course was after they had already thrown the box in the recycle bin. Oh great! Now he was going to have to find a box that would be that odd shaped so that he could return it to the company. Well, he headed to the recycle place to find a box he hoped would work. Before he got to the turn off, he said he prayed and asked God to please let there be some box he could use. He pulled in and there he was able to find this odd, shaped box! There was a lady there and he said to her, "What do you suppose the odds are that I'd find a box with these dimensions?" Her answer, "You must have God on your side!" He then went on to tell her he had prayed about it and look what God did! Isn't it amazing how we get blessed by God? Even when it is something as small as a box.

Well, this got me excited enough that I started asking people to tell me something that God is doing in your life right now, that you were unaware of even needing. The following stories were sent to me by friends and acquaintances who have felt the Hand of God on their lives in their ordinary, everyday circumstances. I hope you are as blessed by them as I am.

First, I want to relate what Mary wrote to me. Mary is a nurse and works in a hospital. She says, "I try to start every workday telling my co-workers that it's going to be a great day! I feel like I'm a messenger to grieving parents when they are watching their child die at the hospital. I gently comment because I lost my son when he was two days old, and I truly understand their pain. My next sentence is, 'You have a lot more memories to deal with, I want you to remember the good ones.'"

God also makes me aware whenever a patient is struggling. I ask if they're a Christian or not. Regardless of their answer, I ask if I can pray for them. In fact, I encouraged one of my patients to get to know Jesus.

Lastly, when I work on Sunday, I will tell my patients, "This is the day the Lord has made, let us rejoice and be glad in it."

I think Mary is finding out that God is helping her through some very hard moments. He is giving her the right words to say, even though she may not know who the next patient will be that comes into her life. God is so good!

Another story comes from a lady I used to work with, whose name is Maureen. She begins her story by telling me, "I saw your Facebook post about what God is doing in your life. There can be no other reason why I am still here today, after the burns I sustained a year ago."

Maureen was in a serious explosion caused by a propane leak. She spent five and a half months in the hospital and rehab. Her son tried to keep everyone up to date on her condition. One week after the accident he recalled, "The surgeon talked about her chest, which was previously thought to be covered in third degree burns. They found that miraculously the chest appeared to be healing itself! No grafts besides a small one is expected on her chest, which is a huge change from any report before this. There is only one explanation for that, and I think we all know what that is! Keep the prayers coming because it's obviously what's helping!"

Maureen is still healing but doing so much better. She says, "The good Lord sent just the right people to help in my recovery!" God is still in the miracle working business. He started healing Maureen's body the moment after the accident. He is still healing her even today. He was healing her chest from the burns and kept her from having even more surgeries than originally expected. God tells us in His Word that He is the God Who Heals us.

Helen sent me the next story. Helen's husband has been diagnosed with dementia. Some days are worse than others for them, as anyone who is dealing with dementia patients already knows. One day Helen was sitting on her front porch and found a moth on the armrest of the rocking chair next to where she was sitting. She says, "It stayed there a long time and didn't move at all. I wasn't even sure it was real at first. Do I think it was a God thing? Yes, I do. Not that I deserved to spend time with the moth, but that I was given the opportunity!"

Here is the part that was God taking care of Helen. This moth was called a Blessing Moth. The reason for that is the way it looks. This moth's wings, while sitting still, are in the shape of a shield. It has a black outline around the wings, but in the center, it has a black cross shape on a cream-colored background. Isn't it cool that God blessed Helen with a Blessing Moth?

Our next story is from Becky. "Despite the situation we are in with David's health at the moment (he is in the hospital, just having had open heart surgery), and feeling like we are drowning in problems, He (God) is faithful to answer prayer on behalf of my health. My DNA test came back, and I am a carrier for Hemochromatosis, but not in danger from it. I just need to be cautious about my iron intake and start donating blood. Praise the Lord for one more thing checked off the list on the way to feeling better!" I am amazed that, amid all that is going on, God took care of one big hurdle in Becky's life!

The next story comes from Betty. She tells me, "God has been leading and guiding me toward the completion of my second devotional book. God is good!" Something else Betty didn't say though was that while she was writing this devotional book, the area she lives in was hit by a storm with winds of 100 mph! I asked Betty to tell me about the storm and here is what she said. "I was very fearful the night of the storm, afraid I would die but, I prayed for safety and strength and God never left my side." There were lots of downed trees, one of which landed on her car! The power outages from this storm lasted quite a long time. On top of that the area was hit with a heat wave, having heat indices in the 100's!

However, God gave Betty Ephesians 1:3-4. "Blessed be the God and Father of our Lord Jesus Christ, who has blessed us with every spiritual blessing in the heavenly places in Christ, just as he chose us in Him before the foundation of the world, that we should be holy and without blame before Him in love." Betty writes this, "Our verse says God has blessed us with every spiritual blessing-how often do I thank

Him for that? He has done so much for me, and I do not appreciate it as I should. I vow to do better from here on."

I think Betty is very thankful and truly saw God perform miracles the night of the storm. I think she will be looking for those spiritual blessings in the future. God was taking care of her, and she wasn't aware until it was over.

The last story I want to tell you about today is truly a miracle. This comes from Jamie, and this is quite a story. I can tell you that I witnessed this one personally and it is wonderful. So, here is her story!

"As I walked into the emergency room, I clung onto Mike just in case I passed out. It had been getting worse and worse! Never had my eyes affected me like this before. I was pretty sure the results wouldn't be good. But little did I know what God had in mind!

Over the last two years, I kept having recurrent inflammation in my eye. Sometimes, it was in the exact same spot, and the treatment didn't seem to be helping. Everyday events like driving, reading books to my kids, or even just trying to see the worship songs on the projector at church brought pain, dizziness, and nausea. Life seemed to be changing in the wrong direction even though I knew with all my heart that God was in control. What made it worse was that now, it was also affecting my cognitive ability and speech.

A few months previously, my eye doctor and primary doctor both agreed that lupus might be the cause for all these symptoms. Blood work was showing that this might be the case. I was then referred to a rheumatologist.

A doctor friend at church examined my eyes and said that one wasn't tracking correctly. One Sunday morning at church, I really wasn't feeling well and just held my head down during the worship service because looking up was too painful. I tried to praise God but the sadness inside along with the physical changes didn't make it easy. A few moments later, there was a time of prayer and an invitation for anyone to come forward to be prayed for.

I knew that God heard my many prayers before, but just felt like I should go. As I knelt down, others came to pray for me and anoint me. Honestly, I only had a small twinkle of faith and told the Lord that I was willing to walk this path if it was His will and if He would get the greater glory, but also asked Him to heal me.

From the moment I opened my eyes at the altar, I could tell things were different! I COULD SEE!

After church, the same doctor friend examined my eyes and didn't see anything wrong! He believed that God healed me.

After that, God sent more confirmation! I went to get glasses that had been previously prescribed and told them the story. My eye exam was great, and I didn't end up needing the glasses. If that wasn't enough, my new bloodwork came back showing that there was not even a sign of autoimmune or lupus! But then came the real Wow Moment...

For years I had struggled with poor night vision to the point that I dreaded ever having to drive at night. Well, God decided that that should be better too! So, needless to say, I can see! I thank God that nothing is too big for Him and that we can come to Him even when we don't feel like it. He meets us right where we're at and knows the next page of our lives. Psalm 139:16 says, "Your eyes saw my unformed body; all the days ordained for me were written in your book before one of them came to be."

We never know what God has in store for us. What a great miracle God did for Jamie!

In this chapter I've tried to give you some glimpses of God and how He is moving. Miracles don't have to be big or earth shaking. They can be small things like a little rain to shoo the goats back in their pen, or a silent moth on the arm of a rocking chair. Look around you in your everyday life and see God! Be open to Him and aware of Him all the time. You won't be disappointed. He's amazing!

CHAPTER 11

Unfailing Love

I'd like you to think for just a moment of the phrase, "unfailing love." The Oxford dictionary defines the word unfailing as, "being with out error or fault, reliable and constant."[1] Dictionary.com says it means, "inexhaustible or endless."[2] I love all these definitions especially when we apply them to our Father, God. I found, as I was looking for information, that the words "unfailing love" are found 32 times in the NIV Bible. It must be something important for us to learn for it to be there so many times!

Some other versions use these terms: steadfast love, lovingkindness, loving devotion, and faithful love. Whatever word you would like to choose, they all mean basically the same thing. My favorite is the inexhaustible definition. God never tires of loving us, He never sleeps or even needs to. He never goes away. These things are a source of comfort and peace to me. I'm glad I serve a God who doesn't get distracted or forgets about me. How about you?

As I started looking at verses with this phrase in them, I found four prominent themes. I'm sure there are probably more and if you wanted to do a study on some of those, I'm sure you would be blessed. I'm going to focus on these four: trust, protection, hope and support, and power.

Let's get started with trust. Psalm 13:5 says, "But I trust in your unfailing love; my heart rejoices in your salvation." Psalm 52:8 reads like this, "But I am like an olive tree flourishing in the house of God; I trust in God's unfailing love for ever and ever." And one more is Psalm 143:8 where David says, "Let the morning bring me word of your unfailing love, for I have put my trust in you. Show me the way I should go, for to you I entrust my life."

Can you see in these three verses that King David trusted God's unfailing love? He was a model for all of us in trust. The definition of trust is a "firm belief in the reliability, truth, ability or strength of someone or something."[3] In this case, Davids' belief that God was worth trusting is very clear. He believes that God is helping him every day of his life, guiding him, and showing him the direction he should go! Not only that but God is allowing him to flourish or to grow in a healthy way.

When we tap into trusting God and believing that He is directing our paths and that nothing happens to us that HE doesn't know about, then we start really growing and getting stronger. Are you getting closer to this every day? I pray you are.

The next theme I found was protection. Psalm 32:10 say this, "Many are the woes of the wicked, but the LORD's unfailing love surrounds the one who trusts him." Another is Psalm 36:7, "How priceless is your unfailing love, O God! People take refuge in the shadow of your wings." And one more, Isaiah 54:10, "'Though the mountains be shaken, and the hills be removed, yet my unfailing love for you will not be shaken, nor my covenant of peace be removed,' says the LORD who has compassion on you."

Isn't it awesome that we have someone to run to when life is falling apart? You can't shake God's love for you. He has always been there for you and always will be. Remember our definition of unfailing? He is inexhaustible! He doesn't get tired of dealing with us. I know this is hard to get your head around. I know me. I get tired and aggravated sometimes when things don't go the way I think they should. But God wants us to come to Him. As a matter of fact, He is unshakeable and has compassion on us. Because of Jesus taking human form, He understands what we go through and that we need A LOT of help! Don't be afraid to run to Him. He'll be waiting! I promise.

Our next theme is hope and support. I lumped these together because to me when someone supports me, I do feel hopeful. I read this recently in a devotional book by Lori Hatcher called, *Refresh Your Hope*. She says, "Every day we have a choice where to look for hope - to created things or to our Creator. The world tells us to hope in money, luck, determination, relationships, skills, and our own abilities. God tell us to look to Him.

The world disappoints us - again and again - but God will never fail us. The hope He offers doesn't rise and fall with changing circumstances. It is solid and secure."[4] Unfailing!!!! I love this. God is steadfast and never changing and because of that we have hope! Another quote from Lori Hatcher is this, "God, our eternal Father, lives, and reigns forever. He will not abandon us, nor will He fail. He transcends time and mortality because He created them. We can rest - unafraid, and hope filled."[5]

Does this mean that we won't have any problems? Does this mean that all in our lives will be rosy? Don't count on it. One of the Scripture passages God gave me for hope and support when my daughter passed away suddenly in a car accident comes from Psalm 94:18-19, "When I said, 'My foot is slipping,' your unfailing love, LORD, supported me.

When anxiety was great within me, your consolation brought me joy." I can tell you from personal experience that HE was supporting me. There were times when I thought I was losing my mind. There were times when I felt lost and alone. When I came upon these verses, I literally copied them down and put them on my desk at school so I could read them during the day. There have been other times in my life that I have written down a scripture and put it in my shoe, so I could say that I'm standing on God's promise to me. Another verse in case one isn't enough, is from Psalm 33:22, "May your unfailing love be with us, LORD, even as we put our hope in you." You know, we have to do what we can, and God will do the rest. We can have hope and support from Him because He says so in His Word!

The last topic we want to look at is power. Psalm 62:11-12 (TNIV) "One thing God has spoken, two things I have heard: 'Power belongs to you, God, and with you, LORD, is unfailing love; and, 'You reward everyone according to what they have done.'" God is able to do what He has promised. If you look at all the promises God made to people in the Bible, you will see some pretty miraculous things! Take Abraham and Sarah for instance, God promised them a son, and it came to pass. Then there were all the promises God made to the Israelites in the wilderness. They were never lacking for food or clothing or protection. King David in 1 Samuel 16 is another example. After he was anointed by Samuel, Scripture tells us that the Spirit of the LORD came on him in power. Think about all the men David led into battle and how successful they were in winning battles for God. He was one of the greatest kings ever, because of God's power.

Let's look at the New Testament as well. The apostles were able to spread the gospel as far and wide as possible for the time in which they lived. Do you think they could have done that on their own? The disciples also performed many miracles among the people where they preached. Saul became Paul through the power of the Holy Spirit! There are so many more examples that I know you are capable of finding.

In wrapping us this study, I just want you to know this, God is all powerful and yet His love for us is inexhaustible love. If we can just wrap our heads around that, oh, how powerful we could be for Him!

So, do you put your trust in His unfailing, inexhaustible love? Do you feel His unfailing protection when life sends storms your way? Do you feel hope and support from God in times when all seems lost? Feel God's power and His unfailing love. He won't let you down. He loves you too much. In fact, He loves you inexhaustibly!

Headnotes

1   Oxford English Dictionary, s.v. "unfailing," accessed August 8, 2023, https://www.oed.com

2   Dictionary.com, s.v. "unfailing," accessed August 7, 2023, https://dictionary.com

3   Oxford English Dictionary, s.v."trust," accessed August 8, 2023, https://www.oed.com

4   Hatcher, Lori. *Refresh Your Hope.* Grand Rapids, Michigan: Our Daily Bread Publishing, 2023. p.13.

5   Hatcher, Lori. *Refresh Your Hope.* Grand Rapids, Michigan: Our Daily Bread Publishing, 2023. p.39.